THE RIOTS

D1331436

WITHDRAWN

Gillian Slovo

THE RIOTS

from Spoken Evidence

OBERON BOOKS
LONDON

WWW.OBERONBOOKS.COM

First published in 2011 by Oberon Books Ltd
521 Caledonian Road, London N7 9RH
Tel: +44 (0) 20 7607 3637 / Fax: +44 (0) 20 7607 3629
e-mail: info@oberonbooks.com
www.oberonbooks.com

A catalogue record for this book is available from the British
Library.

PB ISBN: 978-1-84943-199-6
E ISBN: 978-1-84943-297-9

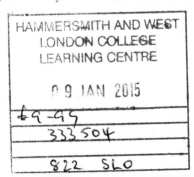
Cover image © Lewis Whyld/Press Association Images

Printed and bound by Replika Press Pvt. Ltd., India.

Visit www.oberonbooks.com to read more about all our books
and to buy them. You will also find features, author interviews and
news of any author events, and you can sign up for e-newsletters
so that you're always first to hear about our new releases.

The Riots was commissioned by the Tricycle Theatre from an idea by Nicolas Kent and first performed on 17th November 2011 at the Tricycle Theatre, London, with the following cast (in alphabetical order):

Barbara Cleaver / Sadie King / Karyn McCluskey Sarah Ball

Martin Sylvester Brown Kingsley Ben-Adir

Man 1 / Sergeant Paul Evans Grant Burgin

Diane Abbott MP / Camila Batmanghelidjh Dona Croll

Inspector Winter / Harry Fletcher Christopher Fox

**Michael Gove MP / Simon Hughes MP /
Sir Hugh Orde** Rupert Holliday Evans

Chelsea Ives Clementine Marlowe-Hunt

Man 2 / Jacob Sakil Okezie Morro

Pastor Nims Obunge / Leroy Logan Cyril Nri

Man 3 / Owen Jones / David Swarbrick Tom Padley

**Greg Powell / Judge Andrew Gilbart QC /
John McDonnell MP** Alan Parnaby

Mohamed Hammoudan / John Azah Selva Rasalingam

Stafford Scott Steve Toussaint

**Chief Inspector Graham Dean /
HH Judge Robert Atherton / Iain Duncan Smith MP** Tim Woodward

Director, Nicolas Kent
Designer, Polly Sullivan
Lighting Designer, Jack Knowles
Associate Lighting Designer, Charlie Hayday
Sound Designer, Sarah Weltman
Audio Visual Designer, Jasmine Robinson
Assistant Director, Ben Bennett
Literary Consultant, Jack Bradley
Casting Director, Marilyn Johnson
Researcher, Cressida Brown
Assistant to the Director, Tara Robinson
Associate Producer, Zoe Ingenhaag
Press Representative, Emma Holland
Production Manager, Shaz McGee
Company Stage Manager, Charlotte Padgham
Assistant Stage Manager, Helen Stone
Costume Supervisor, Anna Bliss Scully

This play went to press before the end of rehearsals

Large and prominent: photographs and moving footage. The most dramatic that can be found of the riots in progress. Shops being looted, shopkeepers defending themselves. Anarchy on the streets of England. Loud surround sound coming at the audience from different directions. Noises of riot. Of sirens. Helicopters. Shouts.

All of this fading out into silence. Theatre is dark. A pause and then:

Two loud gun shots ricochet around the auditorium.

A long beat. Dark and silent.

MAN 1 and MAN 2 on stage but they cannot be clearly seen. It is almost as if they are disembodied voices. They are rioters and, like MAN 3, who comes later, they should be separated from the rest of the characters. They are Other. A world apart from the audience.

They speak throughout in matter-of-fact tones. No heat, no melodrama, just telling us how it is.

MAN 1: I was on Twitter at the time and my trend was on London so I seen everybody talkin' 'bout 'Mark Duggan got shot'. Everyone on Blackberry was like I got a lotta friends from Tottenham so they was all 'Rest in Peace Mark Duggan, Rest in Peace.' Coupla hours later an' I heard they were goin' to protest the next day.

MAN 2: Yeah I basically the same. I was at home an' I see it on Facebook that he'd been killed everyone was sayin' RIP an' that.

Now the stage lights up to reveal STAFFORD SCOTT.

The stage is bright but as the action moves on through this act, as the demonstration moves from the afternoon into dusk and then to dark, the lights gradually dim.

STAFFORD SCOTT: *(His name on screen.)* I was there [for the march on August 6th][1] I felt people needed to be there. What was happening at the time was quite outrageous. A young black male Mark Duggan, someone who was born and brought up on Broadwater Farm, somebody I, I could

---

1. [ ] are used throughout to indicate words added to the transcripts for clarification.

7

have held in one hand from the day I first met him, he'd been gun down on the streets.

There'd been this um misinformation put out that there'd been some kind of shootout that immediately um concerned the community because um we know that Mark wasn't of that ilk. And we know that um most young people, regardless of lifestyle, are not going to get themselves in a situation where they're involved in a shootout with trained, armed, heavily armed, police officers so we knew that that just didn't ring true. It just didn't make sense. And also the fact that the police hadn't had the decency to come to the parents' home to tell the parents what had happened to their son. That infuriated the community.

MARTIN SYLVESTER BROWN: What was released in the press immediately that evening [after Mark Duggan's death] was that he fired at the police. Nobody ever believed [that] for a second… It's not [about] knowing him. Even if you didn't know him, you know nobody shoots at the police in Tottenham. You know, we've got, we've got a history. There's been a history of, of gun offence and even more importantly a history of death by the police, you know, that go way back. You know, there, there's a furious relationship there. There's a long history. A long history and it's all there. It's all documented.

STAFFORD SCOTT: …All this nonsense about [Mark] being a gangster was extremely disrespectful to this family and we wanted to go the police. Um it was almost a tongue in cheek thing. It's been described as a march but it wasn't, there was about fifty or sixty of us. We had some really hastily prepared banners and we strolled to the police station. We didn't march and make noise or anything, and why I say it was tongue in cheek was because we agreed that the women of the group – that was Simone, who is Mark's baby's mother, um she and two other women, and one was her mother, the other a white woman called Jenny who grew up on the estate with Mark – were going to go into the police station and they were going to report that Mark had been killed. And the reason they were going to report that is because tongue in cheek, well, they were saying, well, maybe the police wasn't aware of what happened because the, because the police haven't fulfilled their duty in coming to inform the family.

MARTIN SYLVESTER BROWN: *(His name on screen.)* [Our group, Haringey Young People Empowered] were having a meeting in Bernie Grant's Arts Centre [tackling] issues affecting young people: violent crime, crime against young women, postal code violence mostly trying to create more of a unity because there was postal code rivalries. [The centre] is basically a few minutes from where the [Mark Duggan] protests were taking place. Planning to go, I said to everybody, 'OK, who's coming to the protest?' Everybody was like, 'Nah, nah. I'm not going to the protest. It's going to kick. It's going to kick off. You, you know, you know anger. You know anger.

CHIEF INSPECTOR GRAHAM DEAN: *(In uniform. His name on screen.)* First of all never volunteer for anything…

I'm a cadre trained chief inspector. That is just a flash word for list er a group of senior officers who are trained in public order. We have an on call system and because my girls were away I volunteered to do the weekend so I was on call. I knew that there was a vigil taking place at Tottenham. I'd phoned the senior management at Tottenham er during the day to say, look are there any issues do you want me in, um I'm more than happy to come in just let me know. Cos I was actually cutting my mum and dad's hedge in er West London so I would have to go and get my public order kit. So I said, look, do you need me in before I start cutting the hedge. [And] they said no no, was no issues at the time, everything was quite calm.

MARTIN SYLVESTER BROWN: And then, um, one was like, 'Nah. It's been cancelled because everybody knows it's going to kick off. So it's been cancelled'. I'm like, 'Oh really? OK.' So then I left to go to south London because a friend of mine was going to China for a year.

STAFFORD SCOTT: [The women] went inside the station. The police's response was 'This is a matter for the IPCC [the Independent Police Complaints Commission], we cannot speak to you now.' A very unfortunate response…

The family didn't go there to ask them specifically about the incidents that led up to Mark's killing. What they wanted was formal acknowledgement that it was Mark who had been killed. Because when some family members turned up at the scene on the day um they were told that, that wasn't Mark there. They were told that, that person who was on the floor was from another gang. [But the police told the women] they couldn't talk because of the IPCC.

When the women came out we discussed it. We basically said to the women, 'Look that's, that's not true, they can't be correct, tell them that we want the most senior officer to come here to explain to us why they can't say anything to us and let's see if the most senior officer can tell us something.'

We got there at five o'clock [and] we wanted to be away before 7.30 because Spurs was playing a friendly game about half a mile down the road and we didn't want those crowds converging on each other…

PASTOR NIMS OBUNGE: *(His name: Pastor Nims Obunge on screen.)* I got called by a friend who said 'The march is now on.' I ran…drove, up there to be with the family. So from about five, five-thirty-ish I was there till um the first cars got burned. The intention was to stand there. I, I, I got to meet with the Duggan family and um listen to the challenges they had been through. The, the upset that I heard from the family seemed justified, that they didn't feel they were supported. Um, and I felt that it was right that somebody gave them answers. And if they weren't getting it at home, they had a right to stand where they were standing, with the community, and get the answers they requested.

STAFFORD SCOTT: We asked for this senior police officer about quarter past five, half past five.

Somewhere just before the end of the Spurs game a black police officer turned up. We didn't know at the time that he was reportedly the most senior officer. He got a lot of stick, a lot of cat calls. Not for being the most senior officer but for being a black police officer in that situation.

CHIEF INSPECTOR GRAHAM DEAN: [That]…gentleman, [is] an incredibly er conscientious good lad/er superb bloke. Um he had been there because he was in charge of the football. There was a Tottenham Hotspur home game… So he'd been there all day er and then got called down because [there'd] been problems at the vigil. [He's] a bona fide chief inspector, who actually works at Haringey.

STAFFORD SCOTT: [This policeman] went inside the station. He came out after quite a period of time maybe an hour, people weren't very happy.

PASTOR NIMS OBUNGE: I remember being called by my wife [while I was there] to come home, [and I said], 'There's something that I feel that's about to happen in Tottenham and I want to see whether I can help stop it.' I felt an unrest. There were too many tell-tale signs. Speaking to the community, walking around the community, um, on Friday af- after Mark's death and listening to people's commentary on the scenario there was a, there was just an annoyance. People were annoyed.

STAFFORD SCOTT: So the chief inspector eventually said OK there is a superintendent who's acting up as a chief superintendent and I'll get hold of him and his name is Gurdip Singh. He was out in, I think they said Redhill erm yeah or somewhere near Ilford. They said they was going to send a car for him, a police car blues and twos flashing. Gants Hill [was where] he was, and he'd be there in one hour. It was quarter to eight [when] he said [this]. I actually I pointed out to him at the time and it's the only time I actually spoke to him, and I said you know what, we wanted to be gone a long time ago. It's quarter to eight now it's going to be dusk soon we want to be out of here before night fall comes and if we're not out of here before night fall comes on your head be it.

The stage lights are dimmer now.

We said we'd wait for an hour.

Lights dimmer. Dusk has come.

We waited for the hour.

I should have said part of the reason the women was in the road was so traffic wasn't going up and down. We didn't want Tottenham to go about its normal business when our community was so affected so the road was in effect closed from about quarter past five that, that evening and that becomes significant later on.

It is now turning to dark.

At quarter [to] nine the women, and among the initial group there were lots of young women with children in pushchairs and in arms said look we've got to go, children need feeding, we've got to go. So Simone [Mark Duggan's] um his partner and mother of his children, she said she was going. So we left to go. At that point you could feel the change in, in, in atmosphere.

A map of Tottenham on screen with the police station at its centre.

As the leader of the Broadwater Farm Defence campaign I've led several *(Exhaling.)* oooof several, I must have set a record for marching on Tottenham police station…

OK and, and the way [the police] respond is always the same. They close a part of the High Road, divert traffic round the one-way and send it out via Wood Green. Now on this day, and I think this is down to officers who don't know the area, and it's down to ineptitude, [instead of diverting traffic to go round] they diverted it [so] they let traffic up [and then] there was no way out.

[So two or three officers were] getting the traffic to U-turn and go back these little roads um. They couldn't get them out onto the one-way so they have to send them back.

Sorry for being [so detailed] but it's really really really important.

So the traffic keeps on coming and these guys are there sending them away. Now all of a sudden, where did those officers go? Why did they leave and where did they go? Because as far as I saw nothing untoward happened towards those officers. This had been peaceful.

But [the] officers was gone [and] why they are important is [that] it was their cars on the corner of Forster Road. So they'd gone and these cars are just there. And there was an incident actually much earlier on when we was at the station where a police car obviously responding to some call came zooming through and it it almost looked as if it wasn't gonna stop, so some people took some of those things that were in the road and they they chucked them in front of it forcing the car to stop. It stopped. Officers rushed to the car. They obviously said, look you can't come through here, there's a dead end. Before it reversed some of the kids got some of the fruit from the veg stalls and started to pelt the car with tomatoes and things.

CHIEF INSPECTOR GRAHAM DEAN: If it's only fruit, we can wash that off later. There are high emotions here, members of the family...do we react to people throwing fruit? I wasn't there so I'm not going to say. [But] I can take that car in later and wash it.

STAFFORD SCOTT: [Now] when [the kids] saw these two [unguarded police] cars they did the same thing. There was some vegetable stalls. They took some tomatoes and things and started to pelt it. Pelted it and looked up the road. Where by now there's, there's, there's a much stronger line of police officers. There's forty or fifty officers standing in the road and there's vans behind them yeah? And I'm watching this and thinking well if there's all of you officers how comes you haven't sent a few to turn away the traffic.

The thing is had they done that from the off it would have meant that they would have had officers [in the right place when] we would have been leaving. I've never seen anything like that in my life. I've never seen them employ a policy of leave them to it and certainly not when it comes to my community. It's not about sensitive policing it's about effective policing. And even officers who wanted to be sensitive would of, would have been aware of the, the need to do some of these things.

[The] kids threw a few fruits and things. Nothing happened. They then got emboldened. They decided to get up to the car and start to smash the windows. They were frustrated and the police cars represented a symbol of their frustration so they just went to it. You could see it was in stages. You could see, 'Oh let's throw things at it'. They're not doing nothing. 'Let's smash it'. They're not doing nothing. 'Let's open the doors, let's see if we can get the CS gas canisters.' So that's what they did, they took out everything they could take out of it and they kept looking at the police and it's like, wow, they're not doing nothing. These kids have never ever seen this before in their life. They're used to getting stopped before they do something.

By now it is almost dark.

[So] they steal everything in the cars. Nothing happens. They get emboldened. They push the cars out into the road and it's almost as if the kids are saying, OK, well they must not be able to see us so let's push the car into the middle of the road and they can see us. The police did nothing so they decided to set the car on fire. Set one car on fire.

On stage a bright flare in the darkness.

The police did nothing. They rolled out the other car when they rolled out the other car mmm let me remember, was it on fire or not, no it wasn't on fire it went across the road into a shop, a Kurdish man's shop, a Turkish shop. The Turkish guys came out and started to call the police and say, look, man. Look at this car they've pushed into our thing, and even then the police just stood there. They just looked. The Kurdish guys pushed the car from their shop front back into the road and then the youth went and set fire to the car.

A second bright flare; the stage is now lit with flares which crescendo into the Carpetright fire.

CHIEF INSPECTOR GRAHAM DEAN: The first I heard was when someone, one of the Police Support Unit commanders [who have undergone training in public order policing], one of the inspectors who was actually there er facing some of the disorder phoned me to say are you the, on call er we got problems yeah there's, there's a police car on fire there's a barricade being built and we have we have serious issues [I was] incredibly [surprised]. So I asked the first question which is 'Is this a wind up?' to which he said, 'No this is legit it's happening.' So I said, right, in that case that's fine, I'm on my way.

MARTIN SYLVESTER BROWN: I'm in south London [and I] get a message that it's kicking off in Tottenham. I'm like, *(Claps his hands.)* 'I knew it!'

STAFFORD SCOTT: [We older people were telling them not to.] Absolutely, absolutely. I mean let me be absolutely clear a riot in those situations is the worse thing that can happen for justice. [Tottenham] is one of the last places in London that can afford something like that to happen...

MARTIN SYLVESTER BROWN: So then *(Laughs.)*, so then, um, I get on the train back to Tottenham. And I come down and then, you know, I've got my drum, you know when you go to a protest you bring a drum, and my umbrella. Because I take my umbrella everywhere. And I'm aware that, that day I'm wearing, like, Birkenstocks. You know? Can you imagine? *(Laughs.)* And I'm looking, I'm looking about, a bit too preppy to be honest, with you.

STAFFORD SCOTT: When we went out there, there was about fifty maybe sixty...by the time we left there there were probably 200 maybe a little bit more um but by then we had been there for about four hours and that's the way of demonstrations. They tend to attract people who may or may have not known it was going on [and who later come] along and join them.

PASTOR NIMS OBUNGE: I got the family, the Duggan family, supported them out of the area, because the idea was this was no longer what was intended. I walked with [them], tried to get them on to Bruce Grove and on their way out because, and I, I do remember a member of the family, who may not want to be named, just really upset and crying and just – really really really distressed, and saying, 'This is not why we came, this is not why we came,' um, and so that, that was rather distressing and I could – that was just such an upset – um, but by then Tottenham was ready to start burning.

There were no police officers from Tottenham High Street till Sainsbury's, so people have felt quite frustrated that Tottenham was left to burn. The police have said, no, they were under-resourced. Um, so my question is, could they have done more to resource it earlier on? To nip things in the bud? Those are questions that they will have to answer over their internal inquiries.

INSPECTOR WINTER: *(Plain clothes, name on screen. He is sitting with a cup of tea beside him.)* On – on the Saturday evening, when – when the disorder started, we were in the Tottenham area erm conducting an operation. Erm, and I work in a specialist area of policing to do with surveillance [and] then we were tasked to go to the Tottenham police station to assist them.

It was, it was very tense because… From the information we'd been given, people had been trying to break into the police station to sort of for, for, for whatever reason, to sack it o-or try to set fire to it or, or whatever. So everybody was very tense…nobody was allowed to leave. W-w-we had a small amount of difficulty getting into the backyard because we were – all turned up very scruffy looking – erm in a range of unmarked police cars, some of which didn't have lights or sirens. *(Laugh.)* It's a solid wooden gate and they just wouldn't open it until one of us managed to locate the right frequency on our radio and said, y'know 'Please let us in before they start throwing bricks at our cars!' *(Laugh.)* Ther-there were quite a lot of people milling round but I'm not sure if they were involved in the disorder.

MAN 2: I was at my mate's house in Tottenham so that we could see all the helicopters an' that goin' round. I was a bit worried cos um some-a my family live in Tottenham but like I was a bit excited at the same time.

MARTIN SYLVESTER BROWN: I get down there. And everybody's out. Everybody's out. Everybody, everybody – people I haven't seen in about ten years. Like, 'Woah, was that chap…? That chap looks big now'. I see all these people I haven't seen in a long time.

CHIEF INSPECTOR DEAN: At that stage you could get into the nick. There was [that] chief inspector who was there who'd been on right from the very beginning er for who was geographically based, er in fact he'd been doing the football. I grabbed hold of him, we went out of line of fire into one of the walkways er next to the police station, and said right what's the score what do we need to do. And we had a chat.

INSPECTOR WINTER: W-we literally borrowed equipment an-an-and some…trained officers and formed a serial to go out…erm and stand around the police station… Er – initially there were probably about seventeen of us. Probably two or three hundred at that point.

CHIEF INSPECTOR GRAHAM DEAN: There were two cordons, one with unprotected police officers and no disorder whatsoever to the south. There were people standing there looking. No disorder. No issues. Actually that's quite usual. You'll get, you'll get a nucleus of issues, a nucleus of problems and for any event, not necessarily a riot, you'll get people coming out to have a look at it.

Er and then [there was] a large barricade, people throwing things er petrol bombs being thrown and missiles being thrown to the north...

This was about, forgive me if I'm not specific, but this was about twenty to ten.

MOHAMED HAMMOUDAN: *(Name on screen. He should be separate from the rest of the cast.)* Was getting to about ten o'clock, it was Ramadan round er my er Mum's house. We broke fast, w-we visited family and then I said to the boys, 'Come let's go home'. Er [my two] boys stay with me over the weekends. As, as I's driving up I lived in the flats above what used to be called Allied Carpets but now is Carpetright, not far from Tottenham stadium, [and as I was driving] towards Tottenham the upper end of Tottenham is erm, is where the police station is I actually thought you know. 'There must be something going on,' yeah? There was a load of roadworks *(Breath.)* And the roadworks ki-kind of formed of a cage so it almost seemed like it was like people were caged in. An' 'en I, I, I, got a sense there was something was going. Something innate in me said 'Y'know what I should take the boys back to their Mum's tonight cos it doesn't feel safe. Erm. An' then – because the road was closed off, an' I says 'Ah no I' be fine, I' be fine' So I d- I just drove home as normal, parked up the car, went and picked up the post went upstairs.

CHIEF INSPECTOR GRAHAM DEAN: We've got disorder. But it's fairly big disorder in Tottenham High Road.

MAN 1: When I first actually heard about the riots, I was in my house, with my girl an' I've seen on, on the TV 'Oh riots in Tottenham' I thought 'What!' so I took my girl home an' I've got one of my friends an' I walk down to Tottenham an' I've just seen a good few thousand worth of people on

Tottenham High Road. An' I've never seen such people on any High Road in my life unless I was at carnival. The atmosphere were literally hot. There was so much body heat, there was two fires, everythin'. It looked like a movie, looked like Hollywood come down an' they set up everythin' to look like a mad war zone an' I thought 'Wow'. An' I've seen a good few hundred police tryina diffuse the situation. So I thought – I thought to myself 'Ra!'. There's police there. I'm hundred per cent sure all the police north London were there at the time.

CHIEF INSPECTOR GRAHAM DEAN: We've got a barricade being built, we've got fires being lit er and there's obviously the issue of vulnerable people, and people at risk.

The initial issue for me was let's create some space; let's distance from the police station which was the focus, let's see if we can arrest people er, and get the – get the fire brigade in behind us and we'll do that.

[We] split it three ways. [One] was protection and security of the station. Then, someone to push north, to alleviate the pressure, and to arrest people if possible. Er. And then someone to protect their backs because we could see fires being set. So we knew we were going to have to get the fire brigade in – possibly get the ambulance crews in. So it made sense that they kept the LFB and the LAS – sorry, fire brigade and the ambulance service, came from the south, er, and we would provide a sterile corridor for them to work in.

MARTIN SYLVESTER BROWN: We walk onto Bruce Grove and we're basically, on the front line. Which is strange because I just assumed they'd kettle it off and contain it. But they didn't. They kind of had a line protecting the police station. And after that, anyone – pretty much fair game – you know, anyone can get in and get out and do what they wanted to do. And that's how it was able to spread. I took out my drum and started playing. I just thought, 'Why not?' I just wanted to see what would happen. The police looked over curiously. But I think they just looked at me and thought, 'He's in Birkenstocks. He's not really a threat'… It's funny because since I changed my, my way of dress, I didn't really get stopped by the police.

MOHAMED HAMMOUDAN: I was gonna wake up erm to have something to eat erm because o' Ramadan so you normally wake up a-around three o'clock. An' at about ten to two Amir woke [me] up. I'm deaf in in in my right ear – uh no my left ear, sorry, so I always sleep on my right ear and I don't hear a thing [Amir said], 'Dad there's stuff – the th-th-the fire alarm's going off. Th-th-the smoke detector's going off. There's people knocking on the door'. I said 'Are you sure Amir?' And subconsciously I can hear all this stuff but I thought it was the TV, you know? I thought all this noise was coming from the TV. So I'd woked up and I was a bit dazed. Went and opened the door.

I could see my neighbour. I don't know her name. There's just a whole loada commotion, people knocking on the door, running up and down. And they were saying 'Get out! Get out! There's a fire!'

These strange people with hoods an', an' a lot of them had those kinda Palestinian-sty-style heads – erm masks on or w – scarves wrapped round their faces go up t – y'know, you could see their eyes. Erm… So a – f-first thing I thought I thought y'know phhhw 'I-i-is this real?' Are they really here?' Erm then I thought 'The-the-the-they're t-t-telling to people to leave your door open a's get out'. So that imme-immediately alerted me, thinking 'What, are they here to rob us? Y'ow? Is that – is this like a big ploy? Are they really here to rob us?' *(Sigh.)* So I shut the door.

An' as I shut the door erm I thought 'God this this is serious. This is really serious'. Erm I can see smoke coming through the skirting boards down from Carpetright. There is a fire. And there's so much commotion outside.

It felt like an eternity to wake [Karim] up. I wasn't in a panic. I was more thinking 'I need to get these two out,' yeah? An' I n- I need to do it quickly, yeah? So I was saying to [Karim] 'Listen Baba you need to get up because there's a fire and you need to get get outa here as quick as possible.' An' he was just like tryna put his socks on. I said 'Forget about your socks! Just forget about your socks! Just put your shoes on, yeah?' I said – An' he's tryn – he's tryna put on his – I didn't have any shoes on! I-I-I had a vest on – a-a-and a pair of tracksuit bottoms on and and it felt like an eternity and Amir he were just standing there waiting to leave and he was like his eyes *(Laugh.)* his big brown eyes just standing there and then a' then Karim was taking an eternity. I-i-it was – must have been three-four minutes at the most. It felt four or four five hours. *(Breath.)*

About ten minutes had passed since the time I woke up.

CHIEF INSPECTOR GRAHAM DEAN: By this stage I have two stroke three PSUs who are in the front line, who have been there now at least three hours. Who have been taking flak. I obviously did not have enough protected officers, so that was the first thing I asked for. But of course it's Saturday night, it's school holiday period, so it's heavy annual leave – and it's we had the, we had the football earlier. And of course you had the FA Charity Shield the next day.

INSPECTOR WINTER: I know people have said 'Why didn't you go in there and arrest people?' but it was a case of... At one point there were thirty of us and probably about five-six hundred people causing disorder. If I send five of my officers in to arrest someone who's thrown a brick at us, then either they're going to be surrounded and overwhelmed and it's going to be a more resource-intensive operation to try and bring them back, or y'know, s-someone's gonna get very badly hurt so. F-foremost in my mind is what happened to PC Keith Blakelock [in the Broadwater Farm riots]. I, I don't want anybody to get killed.

MARTIN SYLVESTER BROWN: And at the bottom of Bruce Grove there's a McDonald's [and] there's like, like a Percy Ingle, Superdrug and so forth. That space there, just a bit further down was, I would say the first line where some of the people had built up a line of fire. So basically the police got to try charge that down into that, that box zone. Everyone kind of ran back. And some people were, like, made a volley of bottles and things like that.

We were like, 'Woah'. And some people ran back and some people ran forwards to follow the volley.

I thought [the police] was going to contain the situation. So I was to my friend, 'Yo, what we want to do is, what we want to do is basically move in and move out freely. We got to keep finding new holes to get in and out, to get in and out, so that we don't get kettled. Because I'm not looking to get batoned'.

So we went back. I saw a friend of mine from, from way back. And he was like, 'Madness! Madness!' Yeah, madness! And then we cut down to come back onto Bruce Grove. More people were out. More fires starting. Mostly young people. I know older people were there [but] they threw their bits and then they just went. Young people were just coming out, coming out, coming out. Streaming out into the streets. It felt like a carnival, it felt like carnival but without the aggression. I'm talking about Tottenham carnival now. You're seeing people that you haven't seen in ages. Everybody's out. It's packed like carnival. It was a really strange vibe. Because I'm, I'm here and there's a lot of people, a lot of people I know have got a lot of confidence in each other in the same space. But you don't, you don't get the sense that anything is about to kick off. Bear in mind, you know, there's no, there's nobody actually enforcing. And I know that a lot of time in riots what what you hear [about] is people start turning on each other. Wasn't any of that, not in Tottenham. I heard it was like that in Wood Green. So I'm out of there and I say to my friend, 'Bra, I've never felt Tottenham feel so peaceful!'

CHIEF INSPECTOR GRAHAM DEAN: We came past a supermarket – and I can see [the officers] are on their last legs. It was a hot night, they had hot kit on, body armour, all the other stuff that goes on – carrying heavy shields

I can see that they are suffering from heat exhaustion. I said, go into that store [and get water]. We will pay for that [later. The shopkeepers] were superb. We took some [water and] they grabbed hold [of more] and started running up and down the road, giving them out to officers. Absolutely fantastic to actually see members of the public [doing that] because it felt, not everyone dislikes us.

MAN 1: The riotin' an' lootin' was somethin' that you sit around talk with your friends 'Oh imagine all the shops in the High Road was open, you could go in there an' take whatever you want', thass somethin' you don't expect to happen. So when it's actually happenin' I thought 'Wow, I need to take advantage of the situation cos, this never goin'ta happen again, there's no police, the shopkeepers aren't there, so why not, just go an' take what you want an' come back home'.

I made like a good three trips, took clothes, jewellery, electrics. I even took a-a-a DVD box set of um *Harry Potter* an' I don't even like *Harry Potter*, never wanna see the movies in my life but cos it's there I know it's free so I'm takin' it. I even got a pair of socks, an' I don't even wore the socks yet.

MOHAMED HAMMOUDAN: Time I got out was two o'clock. My ironing board is in the lobby where I always leave my keys. That's all I picked up was my keys yeah? An' I even locked the door behind me, yeah? Cos instinctively I thought we were coming back. I actually thought that fire w-would be like a low-scale fire, be a few carpets burnt. Fire brigade would be here any minute. It'd be fine yeah?

MAN 2: I was just full of adrenaline really at the time. I was just runnin' round I just um thought I'd quickly make some money an' go back home really.

INSPECTOR WINTER: [We were holding the line for] probably about two and a half hours – before some assistance erm started to come. Level Two officers ac-across London – pan London ad hoc serials were formed *(Breath.)* and through the night we had people coming from Lewisham and Bromley and places like that we had people from Essex and Hertfordshire and Thames Valley Police turn up erm which was – which was welcome because obviously before we'd got to the disorder, my team had certainly worked probably about a seven or eight-hour day – so we were quite tired *(Laugh.)* by that point and wearing all the kit and and having to move around so much is shattering!

You've got people coming forwards within a couple of feet of you and they've thrown something at you and they're taunting you erm but you can see that they've got a group of friends and maybe it's a come-on, they're trying to lure you out. *(Pause – lifts cup.)* I think anybody who says they weren't scared *(Drinks from cup and then puts cup on saucer.)* is either lying or an idiot. Erm I mean I've – I've done quite a lot of public order policing. I went to the G8 erm protest in Scotland *(Breath.)* which is slightly different; climate change protest at the G20 in London, er the student protests as well *(Breath.)* erm and, and I've not seen violence on *that* scale, or that much hatred for the uniform – erm as, as seem to be exhibited there. F-foremost in my mind is what happened to PC Keith Blakelock [in the Broadwater Farm riots. [I was] making sure that actually all of my officers are there, sort of counting them every thirty seconds to make sure not one – one hadn't gone adrift, *(Laugh.)* ye-heah it was my biggest priority. It's heartbreaking t- having to watch people's homes and livelihoods being burnt. We don't know if there are people inside those buildings that are on fire or on that bus so actually having to restrain ourselves from rushing in is quite a difficult task cos… One of the key things we do is we-we preserve and save life and property and we weren't able to – w-we certainly abl- weren't able to execute the saving the property aspect of it.

MOHAMED HAMMOUDAN: An' a-a-as I was walking down the corridor it became apparent to me that this was a bigger fire than I anticipated because the whole place was full of smoke, y'know? Th-the staircases they're quite steep – must be at least thirty steps – going down to the erm front door – or th-the the main door. *(Breath.)* So as as we were going down we couldn't see in front of us. We couldn't see who's in front of us. So it was whatever making the de-de-decision whether we would we would go through the smoke or we would g- run back an' go through the other entrance. We didn't know [whether] we were going to the fire. We were just going into like a load a smoke we didn't have a clue. There was people around us, and those other people was still running around, knocking on people's door, telling them to get out.

Those people with Palestinian scarves, they were actually ge- trying to get people out, they're – And – y'know, I quickly put two an' two together a' I thought they were, they were probably involved *(Breath.)* in the disturbances, in the riots, potentially involved in, in setting the fire downstairs to the carpet shop. Some of them got a bit of a conscience and thought 'This has gone too far,' yeah?

Twitter messages begin, slowly, to scroll around the theatre. At this stage they should be faint and fairly unobtrusive.

MARTIN SYLVESTER BROWN: [I was at my friend's house] and we were on Twitter and we got a memo that, basically, there were people in the house that was burning they need support. 'If you can help, come here'. So we left there to go down in the direction of Allied Carpets where we heard that people were being, being escorted out of their houses.

MOHAMED HAMMOUDAN: There were no police around. There was *no* policemen.

CHIEF INSPECTOR GRAHAM DEAN: It had been hard work to get [to Carpetright]. It's actually on a very busy junction. Wide junction – so – Last thing I want to do is get there and get past it. Wide road ahead, wide road behind. So we got there, and then I had to put my resources three ways.

MOHAMED HAMMOUDAN: As we got out the front door, I looked to my right and the place was ablaze. You could feel the heat coming through, yeah? You could feel the heat. I got my two boys over [the road] and as I was going across *(Breath.)* one of the neighbours said 'Could you take my son across as well?' Because they were tryna get some other people out of, of, of, of th-this stairwell you see? They were coughing, they couldn't get out. So I took him and waited and as I was waiting, I'm thinking the fire brigade are gonna come in a minute, yeah? The police are gonna be here in a minute. I was still thinking 'This is gonna be OK. Yeah, it's gonna be OK'. An' then it it kin- it kinda felt really unsafe because you've got your children there y- and you're y-y-you're f- you're kinda feeling really vulnerable, you haven't got your mobile phone, you haven't got – *(Breath.)* you haven't got your wallet, you haven't got *anything*. Everything you just left behind you an-an-and fled out. And erm an' then you've got, you've got, it kinda felt really weird because you've got these people who're just out of the building looking at their their their homes being burnt up and then other people with a sense of euphoria going on. It felt like, it felt like our building was like a trophy.

MARTIN SYLVESTER BROWN: We saw this huge blaze. Huge blaze! The building that everyone's taken notice of. The one that's no longer there. Huge building Allied Carpets – up in flames. The whole building. We were watching it. It was just *(Exhales.)*, it was just, er, an immense flame. Carpetright. But we all call it Allied Carpets. Because, um, it was Allied Carpets for about ten-twenty years. When we got there, we were just *(Exhales.)* in awe. The ash was being blown down on us. We had to cover our mouths. The wind's taking up the ash and the ash is raining down. It looked like boulders but they're not. They're just ash clouds.

MOHAMED HAMMOUDAN: I started talking to, to some of these young people. I said to 'em, 'This is not Aldis, this is not McDonald's, this is not JD Sports, this is a residential area where people live.' Cos at the time other young people, where there was a erm wher- was a tyre shop nearby, yeah? were throwing the tyres *in*to the fire t-to make it fuel even more. And one of these th-th-this young woman who's sitting in, in un-underneath a bus stop was saying to me 'Well you're just trying to prang me up?' Wh-which means you know tryna make you feel guilty. And then there was thi-thi-this this smiling lad erm who said 'Are you you telling the truth? D-do people actually live in there?' I said 'Yes, people *are* living there above the shop. I'm gonna take you to other people who are just in the same situation as me and they're gonna say – tell you exactly the same thing' [and] he actually realised I am telling the truth. Yeah? And his immediate reaction was like 'This has gone too far. It weren't supposed to be like this.' *(Breath.)* An' I said to him 'What d'you mean? "It weren't supposed to be like this?"' He se- he se- he said 'It was supposed to be us and the police and the people who've been oppressing us'. So I said 'Who? Who's been oppressing you?' An' he said 'Well the government, y'ow? The government has been oppressing us'. And then, then, then he said, which is quite ironic, *(Laugh.)* 'e goes 'An' I've gotta get up and fast tomorrow as well'. And I couldn't make out whether he was just a part of the looting and rioting or he actually was a part of setting the whole building a-alight.

INSPECTOR WINTER: [My strongest memory] was in Tottenham and it was a shop owner and his shop was ablaze and all his stock was in there and he'd just purchased some new stock that was in there and um he wanted to go in there and get it out and we had to physically restrain him and tell him that there was no way he could go in there because it would be too dangerous and then he would just be bringing stuff out onto the streets where it would probably be further stolen from him because we weren't going to be able to stay there and protect it um and it's heartbreaking and, and, and when I walked down Tottenham High Road on the Sunday, speaking to someone who'd come here from Somalia, um um you know and he just couldn't comprehend what had happened because he thought he'd come here to safety and now he'd seen something that was akin to what would have happened in his own country in the mid Nineties.

MOHAMED HAMMOUDAN: [I took my children to their mother and then I was driving with my sister] back towards Tottenham an' I started I started looking at the destruction and and the amount of people on the streets and the amount of people carrying stuff, *(Laugh.)* not only young people but people well into their, their you know, their forties wi-wi-with trollies and people walking off with rolls and rolls of carpet they they've taken out of Carpetright, yeah? And I just had to start laughing.

The Twitter messages are now brighter and faster. Telling of spreading riots, the message stream gets faster and faster to the accompaniment of pinging...

MARTIN SYLVESTER BROWN: The road towards Edmonton and Enfield was completely free. And that's when a lot of young people started coming down from Edmonton. And we know they're from Edmonton because they spray graffiti: N9, N18. And this is where they start breaking into shops and taking out things like that.

I'd assume that they're anarchists and the ones that I saw, they were white. A lot of people had their face covered up. But you can, I can, I would say that I would assume the difference between people that I recognise from Tottenham, carrying a specific Tottenham persona, wearing a specific dress and people that, you know, were a bit different. They come with a different tip. So, um, it's a mix. Because you've got the legitimate, you've got the legitimate anger. And then you've got obviously people that jump on that anger.

Fire and mayhem. Carpetright going up. Woman jumping from building.

On the map Tottenham shrinks as the area covered by the maps expands to reveal more of London. New sites of unrest (if possible in order of their kicking off)[2] are revealed, the riots spreading. Expand to map of England showing the spread.

MAN 3: I was at my girl's house at the time yeah? An' I didn't even hear 'bout the shootin' for a good coupla days innit like. I see the riots an' I thought yeah straight I'm gonna get involved in the riots an' that, an' I done my fing an' then I was like 'Why we even riotin?' An' then someone just told me like 'Oh yeah some guy got shot innit' I didn't really care to be honest at the start I didn't know who it was innit, then I see it on the news an' that, an' he was buried in Wood Green innit. I looked at him an' it was like Mark Duggan an' I was like dunno why there's such a big deal about it. I just took advantage of the riots an' done whatever wanted to do innit, that was it.

I was just like 'Yeah man, once in a lifetime thing,' we see it on video games an' stuff like that yeah, might as well do it innit, iss down the road thought 'Why not?' innit, could get lucky or whatever. Shit. I wanted a new iPod an' shit an' I got one innit.

INSPECTOR WINTER: *(Who has his notebook with him which he consults.)* F-f-for the first three days of what was happening – the first day in Tottenham, the second day in Enfield and I think on the Monday we we went to Ealing, erm. O-on that – on the first Saturday, we did a – pretty much a twenty-four hour shift – Had two hours sleep – M-most of us in London don't live in London. We we commute in

---

2. 6th August 20.20: Tottenham police station, Haringey
   7th August 03.00: Wood Green, Haringey
   7th August 18.38: Enfield
   7th August 23.30: Brixton
   8th August 00.29: Walthamstow
   8th August 16.31: Hackney
   8th August 18.30: Peckham
   8th August, 20.07: Birmingham
   8th August 20.23: Croydon
   8th August 21.49: Clapham Junction
   8th August 22.45: Ealing
   8th August 23.42: Camden
   9th August 00.39: Eltham
   (Manchester, Nottingham, Liverpool, Bristol)

from Surrey or Hertfordshire so I ended up sleeping – I think it was Hackney police station – I slept in the corridor *(Breath.)* – I ended up using my body armour as a pillow – for two hours before we were redeployed to go to erm must have been to go to Enfield. We basically followed the level of the devastation. I think it was like twenty out of the thirty-two London boroughs *(Breath.)* had been affected by disorder.

BARBARA CLEAVER: *(Her name on screen plus 'Doctor')* I run the A&E Department [at the Chelsea and Westminster]. I arrived at work at ten o'clock [on Monday] night, and the nurse in charge was like 'Oh gosh, have you heard what is happening?' 'No, I haven't'. And she is like 'There's riots all over London, and it's horrendous, and we might be put on a major incident alert'. There was a lot of tension there, and I was like 'Really!' I couldn't quite believe it. And there was a very senior police officer in the department, and fairly often we have fairly low-ranking police officers, but this was a Sergeant. And I went up to him, and I said 'If you don't mind me asking, what's going on?' And his first words to me were 'Well, we've lost Clapham'. 'What do you mean, you've lost Clapham?' How can you lose Clapham? Well, he was like 'We are no longer policing Clapham… There aren't the resources, so Clapham is now being held by the rioters. The whole of Clapham High Street is on fire. There's looting happening, and we've got no police in there, we're just watching it from a distance.'

CHIEF INSPECTOR GRAHAM DEAN: My experience in Enfield was people weren't standing there to have a fight. People were trying to break into things, they were damaging things and then running away. It wasn't an urban riot, it was opportunist crime. I was in Hackney on I think the Tuesday night, but by then nothing was happening anywhere. And that was incredibly difficult because I've got all these police officers who are ready for anything, in kit, and of course by this stage there's no one to play with. There's no one that wishes to engage police.

PASTOR NIMS OBUNGE: I think there were two [things I saw] that were quite a bit crazy. One was a mother testing the shoes, um, for her child outside the JD Sports, saying, yeah, I would like to see whether this fits. The fact that you're you're, you're looting and you're testing shoes, for-for your child! The other one was, um, was in the McDonald's, I think where they, they went over and started making themselves food. And I just thought y'know, why would you do that? If you're nicking nick, but don't stop over and start cooking.

INSPECTOR WINTER: When you have a serial come from another county, another police force, normally when something like this occurs what-what should happen is you should have a local police officer who goes with them to give them some-some level of knowledge of where they are. Um because of the level of deployments this time that wasn't possible. *(Coughs.)* Excuse me. What happened this time was if they were lucky they got an A to Z which they had to sign for, and if they didn't give it back they were charged forty pounds. Some people do have satnav on their phones and things like that but with these vans, because they're you know, because the likelihood of them being destroyed is quite high, you don't want to put any valuable equipment in them.

I know one police force from up North which shall remain unnamed, when they got told they were deploying here, brought their three worst vans in the hope they would be petrol bombed and destroyed so the Met would have to buy them brand new ones. But the situation is now… Actually they drove all the way down here, those vans have maybe done three or four trips so now the vans are knackered so they're in rental vehicles, they're in Europcar rental vans with police logos stuck on the back and a stick-on blue light, and it's still got the Europcar livery on.

We were aware of what was happening in the rest of the country because we had several vans full of Manchester police officers down here who then had to go back because they'd sent their trained police officers down here to deal

31

with our disorder when their disorder started kicking off there. There was a serial of police officers coming from Avon and Somerset um and then we got told a couple of hours later actually they've had to turn back because there's – something's kicked off in Bristol.

Fade up an audio of the rioters in a loop that gets louder and fades, gets louder and fades, to a background of sirens also getting louder and fading:

Mental bro

What happened last night yeah went mental yeah, went mental

Police got terrored, mate

Took 'em out, mate

An' lissen is gonna happen tonight yeh

Iss happenin' every night for a few days mate, London ain't got shit on us check this now yeah bruv, check this now yeah? Took three thousand police officers yeah just to rush for four hundred of us yeah? See what I-mean they haven't got a shot on Salford yeah, wait till it gets later on about twelve-twelve o'clock yeah – they gettin' fuckin' – Ah shit there's a police goin' past[3].

SERGEANT PAUL EVANS: *(His name, and rank, on screen.)* We came on duty [on the Tuesday]. Bear in mind you've just had three nights of rioting in London. We'd not really had anything in Manchester, at all. On the Monday night *(Coughs.)* in Birmingham it'd all kicked off there. [On the Tuesday] we came in and there was information that there was going to be disorder during the day. We got kitted up in our armour and we deployed into the city, where we all waited. There was three vans in the city, just waited for them, for something to happen. People were like y'know waving at us and saying stay safe tonight lads and y'know and good luck and all that, so you're thinking well you're representing them aren't you, ultimately that's what we're there to do, to protect the decent people of Manchester

---

3. This recording is by Shiv Malik.

and when they're all patting you on the back and saying I'm off home now to watch it on the telly and *(Chuckles.)* you're stuck here but thanks anyway for what you're doing.

Probably about half three [in the afternoon] we started to hear that they were looting the Salford shopping precinct.

SIR HUGH ORDE: *(His name on screen alongside 'Head of the Association of Chief Police Officers'.)* Salford was one of the places where the intensity was probably the worst. And that was within the community. What was the motivator behind that? Part of it was they have some very bad gangs up there who are being dealt with.

SERGEANT PAUL EVANS: There was mass groups of a hundred plus youths who were all covered up in broad daylight. So we then had the drive, under blue lights from Manchester city centre to Salford precinct, which probably took us about fifteen minutes. There was probably twenty-four of us, about two hundred of them initially. We're thinking we can't possibly arrest two hundred people. We had people in the shops, and then we had to get this mob away from there. We went into the estate where we're getting bricked. You don't engage the crowd. [There were so] many of them against twenty-four of us. But they're not all highly trained, they're not all fit, strong, they're not all – we're aggressive as well, you've got to be.

They've not got any organisation. It's a mob mentality, and the mob mentality is [that] they will descend on one person and kill them if they can and that's no doubt what they would have done if they'd surrounded a cop, that's what they did to Keith Blakelock.

MAN 3: I didn't really see any sort of police activity, I just saw police runnin' around like dickheads doin' nothin' innit like. I see on the news in Birmingham an' that like people gettin' nicks an' that if I got hit by the police obviously I would – I would like try an' hit 'em back.

PAUL EVANS: It was horrendous, it was absolutely horrendous, because you've got children chucking bricks at you and

and bits of debris, and then on, if you like stood against the building lines and in the gardens you've got another two hundred people, holding babies in arms, can you believe.

Three words [to describe the rioters?][4] Errrm, hate is one. I know it's a strong word and I don't hate many people but I do feel hate towards them erm, greed. That's what I thought, when they were looting the shops, I just thought, none of you are starving, y'know like they are in third-world countries, no one's starving in this country. So yeah, greed was another thing, and *(Pause.)* cowards, yeah cowards probably was the last one.

INSPECTOR WINTER: [Three words?] That's a difficult one. I would say they were a pack, which I appreciate is more than three words, but um, yeah...out of control, and...scary.

SIR HUGH ORDE: Crikey. Opportunist would be one. Unthinking would be another. Three *(Long pause.)* and frustrated. But [those words] are not joined up.

PASTOR NIMS OBUNGE: *(Sighs.)* Hm. Frustrated. Opportunist. *(Pause.)* And Criminal.

JACOB SAKIL: *(His name on LED and 'Former Young Mayor of Lewisham'.)*[5]

[Three words?] The walking dead.

Interval.

---

4. Note that on these three words, and the ones that follow, there should be pauses between each word. This pause should be particularly long between the second and third word, save for Jacob Sakil, Michael Gove and Iain Duncan Smith who all issued theirs out smoothly.
5. Jacob has a tinge of an American accent.

Throughout this second half MOHAMED HAMMOUDAN sits and watches. He is separate from the rest of the cast. He is listening to these thinkers, these politicians, community activists and rioters, who are all on stage trying to explain what happened.

MARTIN SYLVESTER BROWN: [To describe the rioters] I would use the word, maybe united. Umm that is a word I would use. *(Pause.)* Dissatisfied. And I would say hurt.

DIANE ABBOTT: *(Her name on screen and 'MP for Hackney North and Stoke Newington'.)* I [see what happened in Tottenham] as a classic race riot just like the race riots of the Eighties. Starts with a black person dying at the hands of the police, Cherry Groce, Mrs Jarrett. The police showing insensitivity, obduracy. The community feelings starting to run high. Rumours, heightened rumours about how and why the black person died. A demonstration which tips into a riot. That's a classic race riot. It's the profile [of] the Brixton Riots, it was the profile right up to the Broadwater Farm [riots]. A classic race riot is superficially an anti-police riot, but is actually a confrontation between the black community and the state, the police being the armoured state which they are confronted with most immediately. But a classic race riot actually speaks to a wider and more extensive set of tensions between people and the state, whether it is what's happening in the education system, whether it's what's happening in relation to immigration. [It] speaks to the relationship between black people and the state generally. The police just provide the flashpoint.

CHIEF INSPECTOR GRAHAM DEAN: Er, did I think it was a race riot? D'you know, I'm not convinced it was. Er, I don't know what the catalyst is and because it didn't have the same feel as the Eighties. When I was at Brixton in 1981, when I was at Peckham in 1985, when I was at Broadwater Farm it was clear it was youth, and it was clear that it was predominantly black. I, I, I think a lot of the difference in feel, for me was Broadwater Farm was closed, it was contained, it was locking horns and no one moving. With the disorder we had in Tottenham High Road on the

6th August, there was always an escape route for people. [Going back to your question] I have the luxury of not having to think why – I have the luxury of it's happening here – Graham clear that street. Graham sort it.

LEROY LOGAN: *('Superintendent Leroy Logan' on screen.)* I'm a superintendent in the Met but I'm also part of the Black Police Association executive, so it's from that standpoint um I'll speak about my views.

It's the arena of the Black Police Association to be aware of any sort of critical incident that involves race. So we were monitoring it, um, we were detecting a certain amount of community tension, but nothing to suggest it would develop in the way that it did.

DIANE ABBOTT: Obviously with a race riot you always have criminality. The thing that struck me as slightly different was that because there was this riot on the streets of Tottenham, people saw it and people went up to Wood Green and people went to Tottenham Hale to loot, and what struck me was I switched on my television the following morning, the people were still there looting. People had been allowed to loot for five hours straight in Wood Green and Tottenham Hale. Now, I've said since 'Do you think people would be allowed to loot for five minutes in South Kensington?' No, but they were allowed to loot for five hours in Wood Green.

My view is had the police called in, I don't know, people from Thames Valley or whatever, the police could have closed down the looting and they could have arrested people, they could have stopped it, and I think you wouldn't have had the looting that followed. That's my view.

LEROY LOGAN: I don't think I'll comment on Diane's view cos I've no evidence to that effect. All I would say is um there seemed to be a holding back in terms of the officers seeing criminality, erm the smashing of the cars, the burning of the bus and then obviously that spreading to buildings and looting and so forth but I think the initial damage, the criminal damage to buildings, I think there was hanging back. And it may be just the historical baggage as it were. It may have been a factor for them to hold back, um, not to be seen to be too heavy handed in a very sensitive area.

STAFFORD SCOTT: A lot of people are saying that you can't compare what happened [in August] with what happened in the Eighties. What I really want people to understand is you absolutely can make comparisons, cos the lives of those young people hasn't changed. If you look at all the base line stats – the amount of stop and search that happens are the the the same.

LEROY LOGAN:As a youngster I was quite resentful of the police because of the way I'd been stopped and searched.

I was applying to join the organisation in '82, my father was badly beaten up by officers after a stop and search, and he was fifty-seven, he wasn't the stereotypical person who might be a troublemaker, he was just driving his lorry along and got stopped, they laid into him. He sued them eventually – but, at that time, I was not pleased that had happened to my father. And at that time I was applying to join that organisation, and that had a lot um it was either I continue my application, join the organisation or I become a very bitter person.

You know [today] you're eight times more likely to be stopped and searched if you're black than you're white, um more likely to be strip-searched, and detained for that fact. And of course there is the way in which it's handled, the lack of respect and dignity, we hear about, you know, inappropriate language being used, ugh excessive force.

JACOB SAKIL: *(His name on screen.)* I've been stopped and searched on many occasions. A lot of police officers believe they are the law [and can] do what the hell they wanna do. [They get] away with murder and the young people fester up that anger and they rebel. It's like a never ending circle. [One time] when the police um stopped me they was using cuss words. I understand they tryina speak the lingo but I can speak as intelligent as them. They arrested me, and they treated me as if I'd done something wrong already. And the guys sayin' 'Don't fuckin' play with me, don't fuckin' play with me, I know that you're der der der', I'm like 'What? What you talkin' about?' and at the time I was the Young Mayor [of Lewisham]. When they find out who I were, then they apologised and by them apologisin' they was like 'Would you like a drop home?' I said 'No I don't want anything to do with you guys.'

GREG POWELL: *(Name on screen and, beside it, 'Solicitor'.)*
    There is a legacy for the police at any one moment in time, of how they treat youth generally in the inner-city: the endless stopping and searching; the endless grabbing up and, um, exercise of power. The police would say that very positive, pro-active policing is necessary because of knife crime or gun crime.

STAFFORD SCOTT: If [stop and search is supposed to combat crime in the community], it's the most unsuccessful tactic ever developed. And [now the police] are no longer required to give receipts when they do stop [you]. So that means that they are freer to do what they're doing to these kids before. The issue about stop and search isn't just about the stop and search. The issue is that most arrests that come out of stop and search are what we call knock-on charges. They're not what the person was stopped for.

GREG POWELL: What it creates is a deep reservoir of ill-will and a huge antipathy every client that gets mishandled or mistreated by police, that's their family, that's their friends, um, who then adopt, to some degree, their story and their antipathy. And at any moment, if the social conditions are right, that antipathy can explode into the kind of confrontation, which we saw.

JOHN AZAH: *(His name on screen plus 'Director of Kingston Race and Equality Council'.)* When I talk to my son about being stopped what he says to me is 'Dad it's OK to show me respect once a week, once a month when I get stopped in my, my, my nice car. If three times, four times a week, six times a month I get stopped purely because of my ethnicity, it doesn't, er, it doesn't matter how much respect they show me, I get frustrated. I feel here we go again.' And, therefore, there's a disconnect between what police are saying that 'oh we do our stop and searches very well, we give young people a receipt for stopping them' and [what the youth] are saying [which is] 'hold on a minute I walk the streets like everybody [but] my lived experience is there is a possibility that eight times out of ten, eight times out of ten, I will be stopped because of my heritage and my ethnicity. In 2010, 2011, that wasn't going to be good enough.

PASTOR NIMS OBUNGE: I had a young person say y'know I've just been totally manhandled by police so this is my time to get back, I've heard that.

DIANE ABBOTT: I think with the rioting that cascaded over the next few days starting with the riot in Wood Green, there was that kind of hyper-materialism, that kind of me-tooism. Remember this is twenty-four hour news, you saw these pictures over and over again. People looting in Wood Green. People trying on shoes, people queuing up. You think yeah why not? But also, there was also a mix of [people] because remember as the looting cascaded on over days, by the time it reached Salford the looters were all white.

SIMON HUGHES: *(His name on screen along with 'MP for Bermondsey and Southwark and Deputy Leader of the Liberal Democrats in the House of Commons'.)* On the day the riots came south of the river, Monday the 8th, I was in my office in parliament when I got a phone call from the borough commander of our local police who was literally holed up in Peckham police station unable to get out because quote there were many rioters around the police station. His call to me was to ask if I could do a public call to people to get off the streets, to go home, for parents to find out where youngsters were and so on, because things were not under control. Even though there had been events in north London over a couple of days, the speed and the frequency and the method of what happened meant that effectively the police were on the back foot. And most of them retreated into the major police stations in Southwark, Walworth and Peckham. I learned later that they were told to do that because most Metropolitan police were not trained to deal with public order events. They weren't allowed to go out with batons and shields and headgear only the [trained] people were allowed out on the streets.

I went literally straight away to the studios which are in Millbank and I did the rounds of the studios, I did all the major news channels, [and then] went into where the action was happening. At about the time that the police were beginning to regroup and pull things under control. [When] we arrived in the Walworth Road, uh, a lot of the people who had been there had clearly retreated. So we followed in the wake, literally behind as it were, where the shops that had been broken into…

JUDGE: Stephen Carter. You are 26 years old. You saw bags containing shirts and shoes taken from a store and still in their wrapping, and decided to make off with them. They were worth about £500.

Umang Patel. You are 21 years of age. On Monday 8th August you stole from JD Sports. You were one of those responsible for an overall loss of £170,000 worth of stock. You personally took £220-odd worth of sports clothing.

SIMON HUGHES: Having talked to my colleagues who were there [the rioters were mixed] mainly uh, male, [but] it wasn't all youngsters. There were many over 18 – people in their twenties and thirties, [and] women. I think it's fair to say, given our part of south London, that it was a mix of the community. I actually think that many people would define themselves as mixed-heritage or mixed-race so it wasn't all black.

ANON JUDGE: Ade Alagago. You have pleaded guilty to one charge of handling stolen goods: five mobile phones, two sets of headphones, batteries, chargers and a USB cable valued together at more than £300 clearly looted goods.

You were stopped and arrested just after midnight on Tuesday morning leaving the scene of the civil disorder in Woolwich.

DIANE ABBOTT: The Hackney riot kicked off in broad daylight and [of] the young people that came on the streets, numbers of them swarmed from an estate called the Pembury. The point about the Pembury is that it has got endemic gangs and there had been a police raid on the gangs a few weeks earlier.

SADIE KING: *(Her name on screen.)* I live on Pembury Estate.

DIANE ABBOTT: The Pembury has almost always been a no-go area for the police.

SADIE KING: Nobody has the dream of living in a council flat, but the thing about, the great thing about living on Pembury is it's a really genuinely diverse and tight community. It's got different elements to it. There are people who will say 'It's not like the old days when we used to you know make each other cups of tea' but the bit that I live in anyway, my neighbours are great, you can give them the keys, it is quite an old-fashioned community and that's with, that's young people as well.

DIANE ABBOTT: So there was a confrontation on the streets of Hackney in broad daylight with these young people, and they kind of circled each other. But what happened was, it got dark and all the other people came out, but it was all in and around the Pembury. But that is not coincidence, because the Pembury has gangs and the gangs were at war with the police. But what the police said to me was that as the night wore on you had older people, grown-ups coming out and nicking this and nicking that. So it started off as a young persons' interaction, but older people were also involved.

SADIE KING: It was an outburst. One or two community shops got in the way. But most of it was you know JD Sports. And all the banks were smashed, all the banks along here were smashed, that's not – surely they didn't think they were gonna go in there and take gold bars. [The banks are] not part of the community, they're symbols of things people can't have and things that are making people angry.

DIANE ABBOTT: The funny thing was that it was all kind of co-ordinated and done with texts and instant messenger, and one thing that [was] flying around in Hackney on Monday afternoon was 'Don't touch the Empire, don't touch the Empire'. Because the Hackney Empire, even though it has been partially closed and has had its problems as a theatre venue, it has done years and years of programmes with young people – music programmes, theatre programmes, drama programmes – with young black people. So although they were outside of the Hackney Empire for many hours in the afternoon, because there was a JD Sports two doors up and a betting shop almost across the road they didn't touch the Empire. Which shows that if you can give these young people some sort of ownership and some sort of point of engagement with society, you will begin to find a solution.

SADIE KING: There was no damage to [the] Pembury estate whatsoever.

I went out on the Mon- on the Tuesday to do shopping and when I was coming back from Tescos here and going up Clarence Road, there was loads of people walking up there with brooms. I've never seen so many people, particularly white people walking up Clarence Road. Older black men hang out on the corner and drink cans of beer and stuff and I asked them what [the people with brooms] were doing and they said 'There's some kind of clean-up campaign'. That really kind of jolted me – I thought what you doing? The council have already cleaned up the cars and they – they've just – brand new brooms, they just started sweeping the street for no reason cos it's already been cleaned up. It felt like an invasion like people not from our community have come into our community to clean up. It was patronising.

The brooms was funny it was really funny seeing all these I dunno, yeah, kind of do-gooders coming up Clarence Road with their brand new brooms and I – I remember thinking 'Who's cleaning your house, you know? Maybe some illegal immigrants that you're getting to do it for two quid an hour'.

INTER-LAPPING JUDGES VOICES: Michael Gillespie-Doyle. You are only 18. You went into Manchester knowing that the disturbances were under way. When you saw that the store had been broken into by others, you took your chance with your accomplice and went in and took goods.

Mohima Khanom. You are 23 years of age. You went voluntarily to the scene of civil disorder. You say you followed the example of others. You helped yourself to almost £9,500 worth of stock from Carphone Warehouse. Your naked greed is breathtaking.

Mary Boyd. You are 31. You were in the city centre doing what you usually do there – that is go drinking with friends in the street. You saw lots of people running past, and when you came across an abandoned bag containing alcohol, cigarettes and a mobile phone.

CAMILA BATMANGHELIDJH: *(Her name on screen, plus 'Founder of Kids Company'.)*

I actually wrote three weeks before the riots to Downing Street saying that I felt things were going to blow up at street level because I could feel it and it was coming from the kids. They felt this sense of wanting to take revenge.

Central government was presenting large chunks of these inner city environments as spaces where lazy, benefit acquiring er population were letting the rest of the nation down. The minute you start describing the poor as the lazy you split off a large section of society by er humiliating them. The underclass was described as 'amoral'. And this is very important in terms of how people ended up behaving. If your membership to mainstream society doesn't produce a reward in your eyes, then why have it?

It felt like government was constantly saying 'You're benefit scroungers, we're gonna cut your er accommodation situation', [the Education Maintenance Allowance] got cut and so on [and this] in the context of unemployment that was running at one million for young people.

SADIE KING: The thing that I really object to is the way young people are treated in Hackney generally by...the police... They have very fast quick-fix policies that are quite brutal, um the main one on Pembury being dispersal zones. Dispersal zones have been going for about five years. They put notices up they have them for particular fixed periods and what it does is it gives the police extra powers to stop and search if you're under sixteen, if you're out after a certain hour which isn't very late, about nine o'clock or something, they can ask you to go home, can escort you home or take you to a place of safety. Sometimes they decide to do it in the summer which is awful. If you see the flats [on the Pembury] there um you know, they are nice flats but they're tiny. If you've got a couple of teenagers living with you how can you possibly keep them in from nine o'clock on a summer's evening. And they do not have back gardens there's no facilities. So the street and [the] communal areas is their space. The kids are so used to [dispersal zones] now they'll separate. They'll go, 'OK we're not allowed to stop if there's two of us so we'll separate when we see you'. It creates [in] kids of like 10 this kind of anti-state, you know, anti-police culture, and they see themselves as labelled and they see the police as there to interrupt them.

STAFFORD SCOTT: They talk about a feral underclass. I think it's a mindset. It's a mindset that says that we are treated unjustly, we are never gonna get respect, we're never gonna get the dignity that we want, so let's go and just take the things that we want. And there are people out there who have their own anger and frustration at the police, and at these institutions that completely fail to deal with them. And the truth of the matter is it wasn't a race thing. We saw when the Turkish community came out to protect their things, we saw when the Sikhs came out to protect their things – it was the haves against the have nots.

CAMILA BATMANGHELIDJH: [The disrespect is] insidious. It's drip drip drip and then I think [Mark Duggan's] death was the tipping point.

STAFFORD SCOTT: In a three-mile radius four people have died at the hands or whilst in the custody of police officers. None of those four people were ever found guilty of committing any crime. The nearest they got was Joy Gardner who was an overstayer and they wrapped thirty feet of masking tape around her face. Nobody ever got charged for that. Nobody was ever held to account for that. We're a community that doesn't expect justice.

MICHAEL GOVE: *(His name on screen plus 'MP for Surrey and Secretary of State for Education'.)* The first thing my wife said [was] that the riots were like one of those Rorschach blot tests in that everyone sees that – what they want to in them. So that um, um one person who's got a particular view of society, and who believes that the principle sort of um thing that's wrong with society is the unequal distribution of opportunities of wealth, will see the riots as a reaction against that. Someone else, who's a stern old-fashioned Victorian moralist who thinks that it was a mistake to get rid of the cane in schools will say see what happens now you've got rid of corporal punishment and so on. So they were in that sense um er an opportunity for everyone to rehearse positions that they already had.

I think the rioters were a vicious, lawless and immoral minority. By definition, if you're um, if you're prepared to destroy people's property, if you're prepared to engage in violence like that, that's by definition without wanting to sort of engage in exercising tautology, vicious and lawless.

STAFFORD SCOTT: [We saw] what's happening with those politicians who just took and took and took and took. And we saw that only a few of them got charged even though loads of them broke the rules and then broke the laws and of those who got charged, they get silly sentences and come out after a quarter of their sentence.

GREG POWELL: *(His name on screen plus 'Solicitor'.)* Some of our regular clients, if I can describe them in that way, got arrested. But also because we're in north-west London and the south London cells became full, they migrated a number of prisoners from south London to the local Wembley-Kilburn police stations. And one of my colleagues was a duty solicitor on that particular day and so we picked up a – a group of clients, who really belong in south London.

I anticipated straight away that it would not be normal, because I remember acting for people in the 1980s – in the riots then. Experience tells us that what happens almost by reflex, is that the criminal justice system reacts in a very punitive way to send out a very clear message that you shouldn't be engaged in rioting because you get locked up.

STAFFORD SCOTT: What people need to understand is that the behaviours that we saw out there are the same behaviours or the same kind of mindset that helped to create some of those British suicide bombers. It's borne out of that same frustration, that same sense of being dispossessed and marginalised – and that was what makes them feel compelled to do something about it. Those kids were, to all intents and purposes, they were suicide bombers. And in our community they have been imploding as opposed to exploding. And on that Saturday, they exploded. So telling these kids stop what you're doing or we're gonna give you longer, more draconian sentences is like saying to someone strapped with a bomb, stop or I'll shoot – it doesn't mean anything. It reinforces their belief, it reinforces their cynicism.

LEROY LOGAN: I'm really concerned about the disproportionality of the convictions but unfortunately the Court of Public Opinion was so devastatingly bad. People were angry. Areas right across London and the UK or England anyway, were being torched.

I think the Justice System has to review what has taken place. I was being interviewed by some French TV [and when] they asked, 'Why have you gone so excessively long on the punishment?' they were actually um [citing] Ed Milliband's [hard line]. They couldn't believe he's seen as a socialist, left-winger and he's falling in line with the right wing.

I think you have to judge every case on its merits. Um, you know as a – as a superintendent authorising further detention for someone, I look at that individual case, I look at papers, I look at what investigation is carried out and I judge according to that. If it's a group of people, I'm still judging each one individually I don't judge it collectively.

HH JUDGE ROBERT ATHERTON: *(His name on screen followed by 'Sentencing remarks in Manchester on 18th August 2011'.)* David Swarbrick. You pleaded guilty at the first available opportunity to an offence of burglary of Quality Save, a shop on Oldham Street. You were arrested at 9.40 p.m. and were found to have stolen a number of items of cosmetics. The value was low. You had seen the incidents in the city and took advantage of the situation. You are almost 26 years of age.

DAVID SWARBRICK: *(His name on screen. In prison, he must be visibly set apart from the rest.)* Thursday 6th October 2011. HMP Manchester.

Dear [Tricycle Theatre],

My name is David Swarbrick, I am 26 years old. I was caught up in the Manchester riots, on my way through the city centre.

I ended up blocked in by police barricades + everywhere I looked or turned there was pure pandemonium + chaos. I witnessed a whole, broad range of members of society kettled in, corralled together – old people with shopping, students, all ethicities [sic], man, woman, kids, some with ski mask, some just with drinks, from pubs. While locked in Piccadilly Gardens, I saw dozens of shops of varying size and expense just open, doors gone, windows smashed, shutters peeled off fronts, like giant sardine cans. I entered a branch of a well-known brand. Subsequently, I was caught red-handed inside + apprehended, charged as entering as a trespasser + stealing 'things'.

JUDGE ATHERTON: I have read the letter which you have sent me and the Pre-Sentence Report. Your attitude towards your offending is to feel regret for the embarrassment which you have caused your family and the citizens of Manchester, yet on the other hand have described your general offending as being 'an occupational hazard', your comment to the police was that 'It's no big deal, it's only a bit of moisturizer'.

DAVID SWARBRICK: I was told under normal circumstances that I would have expected to receive a six-month sentence for a commercial burglary of a value £2,000 or less. At Crown, I was with eight other defendants in the dock. We were each sentenced one by one.

JUDGE ATHERTON: In my judgment the appropriate sentence after a trial would have been thirty months imprisonment. I reduce it by one third to twenty months and the suspended sentence will take effect consecutively making twenty-four months in all.

DAVID SWARBRICK: Twenty-four month = two years.

DIANE ABBOTT: I know that the sentences are very controversial, but I would think that the public would expect the sentences to be exemplary. I generally think it is not for politicians to second guess the sentencing by the judiciary in the context of an urban riot [I would expect] the Courts to seek to impose exemplary sentences. I think the public would expect them and excesses are dealt with under the Appeal system. That's my view, but I know that is not the view of many people on the Left.

PASTOR NIMS OBUNGE: [When people say that the British public demanded punitive sentences], I'd like to know when they spoke to the British public. Are we talking about journalists, the *Daily Mail*, or some of the other newspapers, say [is] the word of the British public. Y'know what is, who is, the British public? The media has had no social conscience or moral conscience because there is a a commercial responsibility. And so, the definition of the British public always leaves me wondering who defines the view of the public. I, I think that maybe we should have some community based punishments, rather than incarceration, um, in some cases.

JUDGE ANDREW GILBART QC: *(Name on screen plus 'The Honorary Recorder of Manchester on the 16ᵗʰ August 2011 at Manchester Crown Court'.)* David Beswick. You are 31 years old and in work. You took your car into Salford to go and watch the disturbances at something like 7.00 p.m. You were still there at 00.40 a.m. You knew that several stores had been attacked and looted. In your car was found a 37-inch television taken from one of the stores.

OWEN JONES: *(His name on screen.)* Many of the MPs who, er, stood up to demand the, um, demand tough action themselves three years ago had pillaged public finances to, um, to buy the same sorts of widescreen TVs that were being carted out of shops by looters, in an, admittedly, more disorderly fashion. Gerald Kaufman, an MP, stood up and demanded action was taken. And he claimed for £8,500 for buying himself a television set.

JUDGE GILBART: You told the police that you were looking after [the television] for another for payment of £20. In other words you were the means by which that stolen TV would be taken out of there. I regard it as a cynical offence by someone who knew exactly what he was doing.

You do not have a bad criminal record, and no previous offences for dishonesty. True it is that you have recently lost your mother. [But] you stood and watched crime going on for some hours, and then played your part. There must be a custodial sentence. As you admitted your guilt at the first opportunity, the sentence is one of eighteen months imprisonment.

CHELSEA IVES: *(Her name on screen plus 'HMP/YOI Holloway'.)* 10th October 2011

Hi my name is Chelsea Ives and I have recently just turned 18. I'm the girl that got shopped by her mum due to the riots. I read your article in the prison newspaper so I thought I'd share my veiws [sic] on the things that have involved me for your theatre and because the whole country knows who I am. I think it's terrible what the news have said about me, they have made it look like I'm a disruptive low-life teenager from a council estate. The public seem to automatically place me in an unnamed catorgory [sic] for thick, low-lifed individuals which is not me at all. I havn't [sic] even had the chance to speak for myself. It just feels like I shouldn't even have legal advice, because it seems the Judge has already made up his mind about my sentence due to the help and support of the media. The public just need to know I'm only accountable for my actions and not everyone else's and that I am sorry. Chelsea Ives.

HARRY FLETCHER: *(His name on screen plus 'Assistant General Secretary of NAPO'.)* I received phone calls from people during the period, I suppose we're talking 14th August onwards when they started court sitting at night and at weekends, that there were insufficient staff to provide information for the courts about the background and motivation of individual offenders.

My view has always been that the court sentence each individual based on the individual circumstances of that case. And they clearly couldn't have had sufficient information to determine whether the motivation was socio-economic, whether it was purely opportunistic and greed. The courts were also under tremendous political pressure to deliver swift justice.

MICHAEL GOVE: I can't know quite what the motivations were of all the people who became involved. It's undeniably the case that er there is a um somewhere in the human soul there's um a – the capacity for enjoyment in violence and destruction, wantonness. It's undeniably the case that there are people who, um if they have the opportunity to um engage in consequence-free violence and destruction will do so. So if – if you feel that the bonds of restraint aren't there, you'll do so. Some people will do so believing that they're animated by a – a higher cause, a higher purpose, but in fact they're just slipping from the rational into the emotional.

[My three words to describe the rioters?] Tragic lost souls.

MAN 3: Everyone was there man like it was black people, white people, everyone – everyone was there man, there was no, there was no – you can't blame anyone, everyone was there innit like. If something there for free you take it innit. I dunno why people try to lie about it man. If somethin' there for free you take it. Everyone was there man, dunno why – everyone was there man – everyone took part in it.

GREG POWELL: I think [the courts and the government] don't necessarily think through to cost benefit. If you want to look at it in purely managerial terms it would probably be better at the lower end of criminality to give people suspended sentences in order to deter them from future offending. And couple that to curfews, if you want to keep them in at night. And/or community payback, if you want them to do something on behalf of the community. A much more expensive solution is to give people immediate, fairly lengthy custody.

There are very strict limits to how much their individual identities matter. And that in its own way is a bit of a shock because you're being told, really, that you don't matter as a person. You're going to get a sentence which is much greater for your particular criminal act, than you would have got if you'd done it individually. And you're also being told that your personal identity is of no account. So that's liable to make you a bit bitter.

MAN 1: Like I said I knew I could make myself a good few hundred pound. I been applyin' for jobs the past year an' I ent got nothin'. An' it's not come, it's not come to the point where like I've got rent to pay or whatever but my Mum is not on no big money paying job, she can only give me – she can only buy me a certain amount things. An' my Dad's not here to help. It's just me an' my Mum by ourselves an' there's only so much she can give me so everythin' else I've gotta go out an' get myself. So if I know I can make myself extra money then why not?

HARRY FLETCHER: I do think that there is evidence that some people who had not been in trouble before, uh, got carried away. But I remember one kid shouting at a reporter 'We're getting our own back'. And I think that was related to the fact that a lot of the people who were rioting came from relatively deprived backgrounds where obtaining a 32-inch plasma screen or trainers that cost a hundred and fifty quid weren't possible unless they stole them. Yet the idols that they were supposed to look up to like footballers on a hundred thousand pounds a week and popstars had all these things. That's why I feel the courts had to have the information about individuals, because the motivations are very, very complex and different. Certainly some kids purely exploited the situation to get things for nothing, but others, er, were quite, er, definitely from deprived backgrounds, were excluded from mainstream society and saw it as a way of getting, to get goods they couldn't get in any other way.

IAIN DUNCAN SMITH: *(His name on screen plus 'MP for Chingford and Wood Green and Secretary of State for Work and Pensions'.)* The police do have a role to play and the criminal justice system has a role to play. They have to leave a very strong signal that first and foremost the criminal justice system will be there should [you] make that conscious decision to transgress it. [But] sentencing like that only ever has a short term effect. Er, it's like applying electrodes to somebody for a short period of time. It causes you immediately to recognize something has happened for the short period of time you will remember that that was painful [it] works at the moment of contact to get back control and to send a very swift signal that actually the justice system will work and you will I'm afraid pay a penalty for what you chose to do. [But this] will work only so far as there's something else happening behind it.

MAN 1: The way I see it – London in particular, north-east and south London, are majority workin'-class people. Middle-class and upper-class people will not be materialistic because they've got money, they work decent jobs, or they was born into a wealthy family whatever.

When I was young, having a pair of trainers in school was the 'in thing', or a nice jacket, cos like I said, we're all from – we're in a working-class area so if you turn around in your I dunno hundred pound trainers an' say 'Oh look at these what I got yesterday' people gonna think 'Ra this guy's top guy in the school cos he got the best trainers'. So that can in a way put you in a different – different calibre or class whatever in your school area. Think yeah that's the guy with the expensive trainers, then you got this guy over here with some no-name trainers from Shoe Zone or somethin' so yeah, havin' a good pair of trainers around here is a way to bein' different calibre compared to everyone else.

If I had money to myself put away in a bank or wherever from workin', then why do I need to go out risk myself gettin' nicked for lootin'? If I'm earnin' from workin' I don't need to go out an' do it again. If I had a job I wouldn't have wanted to do nothin' cos I'm not gonna spoil my chances for the future cos I know that if I get arrested an' I get, an' I get a criminal record, me tryina find a job again is gonna be even harder than it is now. So that was exactly why – why I went an' done it.

JOHN MCDONNELL: *(His name plus 'MP for Hayes and Harlington' on screen.)* Society has created a society of looters at every level: MPs fiddling expenses, bankers with their bonuses, corporations not paying their taxes, and all this was, was kids with the same moral values that have been inculcated in society motivated by the same level of consumerism, um coming out and seizing their opportunity. [And how] are those moral values transmitted to the kids? By example. I think [they're] a-absolutely indoctrinated with consumerist values. Under the Welfare State at least there was some feeling of solidarity and sharing and, yes, to use that expr- phrase 'being all in this together' but that's gone now.

IAIN DUNCAN SMITH: It is difficult to get jobs but there's no magic wand to say 'I'll tell you what let's make jobs easier to get and let's have more jobs'. The fact that lots of people have to commute longer distances in these cities for the very simple reason which is there are no jobs near them that they can do, they have to go somewhere else. So one of the things about restoring balance in these um areas, is that you also restore the likelihood that jobs will return to those areas that are viable and doable by local people.

OWEN JONES: In places like Tottenham today there's thiry-four unemployed people for every vacancy. Erm, and what's on offer often is low-paid work in the service sector – supermarkets, for example. Um, and that's not work people necessarily aspire to. People don't feel that same sense of pride working in a supermarket they might have felt in the work which used to exist. They call it 'The Hourglass Economy', where middle-income, skilled jobs, not just in manufacturing but in a whole range of different industries, all disappeared, um, in the 1980s at a very dramatic speed. And low-paid, service-sector jobs expanded at the bottom as well as professional jobs at the top, which most working-class kids have no access to.

There used to be a structure [for working-class youth]. You could leave school at 16 and go into an apprenticeship, which was respectably paid and [it] was a gateway to a life where you could be sustained by work. And that disappeared [and it] left a vacuum. More broadly what happened was [an] explosion in inequality. I mean,

Britain was one of the most equal Western societies in 1979; it's one of the least equal now. There are people in communities, like Hackney one of the poorest boroughs in the country, in which the poorest live alongside the richest. It's almost like being taunted: these are lives you will never have.

SIMON HUGHES: Don't give up hope that actually paradoxically, we might end up at the end of this government with a smaller gap between the rich and the poor than we did at the end of the last government.

[My three words for the rioters?] Impulsive. Reckless. This is not a word it's a phrase, there probably is a word but, um, uh, responding to the excitement of the opportunity.

IAIN DUNCAN SMITH: [My words?] Dysfunctional, criminal and lost.

OWEN JONES: One in five young people [are] out of work, um, with a sense that there's no future to put at risk. And if you only have a tiny fraction of young people who feel they have nothing to risk responding in this way – that's enough to bring chaos and violence to the streets of our cities.

JOHN MCDONNELL: I think the riots were an inchoate response to people's anger in society. There's a feeling of anxiety. All. All ages. Young people [are] just as much victims as the older ones. [And] where do those kids go when they come home? Well they go on the street. And who are the other people on the street? Other kids. So do they form gangs? Yeah maybe, but informal associations because they're out there. Where do you go when you've seven, nine of you in a two-bedroom property?

STAFFORD SCOTT: They are young people that live on the margins of society, and are now being told that they have to pay for the fat cat bankers who are still paying themselves crazy bonuses here is is an absolute awareness [of this amongst them.] They're not going to sit down and and watch *Channel 4 News* and get into all the detail for that, but they have an awareness – there is an absolute awareness that they lost their EMA.

JOHN MCDONNELL: The the EMA cuts are significant. There's a feeling of the ladder's kicked from underneath [young people]. One of our campaigns was to get people to aspire to go to university, and this just undermines that whole campaign. The second thing, the EMA was critical for them staying on in some form having that undermined is a real kick in the teeth.

[As for our youth services and youth facilities,] gone.

In the last Tory government, Tory councils, they cut the park wardens and they cut the youth services at the same time and they closed the youth centres so the kids streamed into the parks, there was no control erm lots of vandalism, we even had a murder in one of our parks. We rebuilt that, reopened the youth centres, and had some youth workers back on the streets again. [And now] they've even cut the park wardens so we're back to square one where areas have become no-go zones.

DIANE ABBOTT: [If I was the government] I would make youth provision statutory; the point is that youth provision is non-statutory, so whenever the government has to make cuts, that is the first thing that goes.

IAIN DUNCAN SMITH: Do you think that certain things that are important should be ring-fenced and sent down to councils without any opportunity for them to change it? There's no magic wand that says this is the right way or the other way, I mean the last government did a lot of ring-fencing of stuff and that leads to quite a lot of inefficiency. My sense about this is much more important is to get councils to recognise the importance and the seamlessness of certain things that have to happen, so things like youth services that helping kids are important because they help councils and they help the area in due course and that benefits the council.

LEROY LOGAN: We always have that summer madness in August, we always have that peak where young people invariably get restless, they get bored, you know and you've gotta give them something to do. And unfortunately through the recession and the cuts one of the biggest victims of that is the youth services. I know that a lot of boroughs have cut intensive supervision for those who are vulnerable, or at risk or even dangerous, and if you don't have those resources keeping those people engaged in activities and you know watched it, just develops this sort of powder keg and it just takes one spark and it explodes, you've seen that.

MICHAEL GOVE: I haven't seen anyone arh, um, erm, er produce evidence to suggest that um the lack of um local authority or other youth services has played a significant role here. I think it's easy to say the answer is more state spending on x or y, the question is why aren't there other er why aren't young people joining or involved in other organizations that can give um er purpose and enjoyment to their lives. In other words, whether it's the um scouts or the cadet force or other activities, one of the questions that we need to ask is to what extent are there cultural or other barriers that prevent people from becoming involved in other activities.

GREG POWELL: The Labour Party remains the single largest party which would, um, pretend, at least, towards some wider social engagement amongst many of its individual members. But I don't see it at a local level successfully reaching out and engaging and drawing people in. I mean, what struck me about the massacre in Norway, was that it seemed to me unthinkable – that comparable numbers of young Labour Party supporters [would] gather in a social setting to discuss the future of politics. There seemed to be something happening in Norway, amongst Norwegian youth, which does not have a parallel here. You wouldn't find a hall full of people to massacre who were future potential leaders of Labour...because they don't, I think, exist.

I don't think [the riots] was an 'accident' [waiting to happen]. Um, is it a, is it something which we can expect to happen again? I think 'yes'.

IAIN DUNCAN SMITH: [The inner city] came knocking.

I don't [blame] the last government particularly, I blame a whole series of governments who have failed to recognise that what was going on underneath our nose was the creation of a subculture and that what we were trying to do without realising, perhaps even intellectualising it, but what we were doing was ringfencing it saying as long as that doesn't break out anywhere else then we're sort of OK.

That's why I think the um, um violence and sort of criminality that took place on those few nights that exploded onto the streets is, whilst bad and desperate and terrible, is also in a strange way quite good. Er because, and I don't mean that glibly I simply mean because it is a strong reminder er that we er have to get this right and we have had a wakeup call to tell us you know we've got to a point now where this is gonna happen again unless we start to deal with it.

SADIE KING: [Do I think anything good came from the riots?] Yeah I think it's raised the issues. It's, it's opened up… the conversation about politics and it's opened up the conversation for once about the police um locally. I think that lots of people who wouldn't have said anything about the police are starting to say these young people feel intimidated, they are being um harassed, they feel like they're labelled. It's [as] if living here you're labelled as a gang member, even if you're a child.

Lost, angry…um… *(Pause.)* confused would be [my three words to describe the rioters].

OWEN JONES: [Mine would be] Faceless. Dehumanised. Unexplained.

If you want to make sure [the riots] never happen again then we need to understand them.

HARRY FLETCHER: [If I was the government, knowing what I know, fearing what I do, what would I do?] It would be, kind of not wanting to sound too pompous, it would be to adopt a Keynesian model, instead of cutting everything to pieces, you basically invest in public works, you create employment for people.

STAFFORD SCOTT: If I was in government I would recognise that we have a lot to learn, and the first thing we needed to learn is we've got a lot to learn. I would go around and I would identify authentic voices of those communities, because part of the problem is that government listens to who it chooses to listen to.

KARYN MCCLUSKEY: *(Her name on screen plus 'Co-director of the Scottish Violence Reduction Police Unit'.)* What happened in the riots was absolutely criminal, but I tell you what would be more criminal, if we missed this opportunity to really change, to set a really brave path, so that other countries are coming back to us in ten years' time and saying look what England and Wales did in response to this, look how they've changed.

It was fatal, fatal to take away the ring-fencing [around Sure Start]. We literally spend a huge amount of money on public services and a whole range of other things, in the UK. We need to need t-t-to talk about where actually we should invest to get the better return on our money. [A Nobel Prize-winning economist] said, for every pound you spend [in the] early years, between nought and three, you will have to spend fifty or sixty pounds at the age of sixteen to get the same effect. Makes perfect sense to me.

[In the 1970s] Denmark realized that they were falling off the cliffs and [they] fundamentally changed the way they did childcare. They developed what they called pedagogues who go into families and support children under the age of seven. Their outcomes are spectacular, y'know, and they support every family. Wouldn't it be a great strapline for the UK if the UK was the best place in the world to bring up your kids?

STAFFORD SCOTT: I don't think anything good ever comes out of riots. Ever. I think in some situations we had public inquiries and something good came out of those public inquiries. The only time we make any stride with race relations is on the back of an inquiry. Every inquiry always comes back saying yeah what they said is true, always does so it's the, the only thing that we find helpful.

[My three words for the rioters?] Frustrated, angry, and British.

The reason I say [British is because], this was a really British thing. In the Eighties [riots] there was lots of Caribbean involvement, lots of Jamaican involvement. [For these recent riots] the Turkish kids [who] were out there either came here really young, or were born here. The black kids who were out there – the majority were actually born here. [These kids were] giving voice to their disaffection and dissatisfaction with life in this country. [Their] riots weren't imported, they were bred here. It was a quintessentially English riot.

MOHAMED HAMMOUDAN is alone on the stage which is dark save for a spot on him. A reprise of some the riot noises but much softer, fading into nothingness.

MOHAMED HAMMOUDAN: The thing that really kind of got to me when I got back to to, to the fire [was] all these people taking photographs. My house has been burnt down and [they're treating it as a] a marker in his – in history. Was almost as if they just *need* to be there. They needed to catch the moment.

It's er – it's unbearable to think that you live relatively speaking, in a really affluent country where you've got y'know a huge amount of resources in public services shrinking but still y'know, relatively speaking to other countries huge – and the system just broke down. The system failed us, yeah? I'm all for people protesting, I'm all for people giving their views across, and holding people to t-to to account. But I just feel like y'know, the whole emergency services were just caught on the back foot, y'know. It's just like they had, they had no plan.

I feel, I feel empty yeah. *(Laugh.)* You have to start a new chapter without having erm the the seeds there from the past. You, you can't show people things any more. I can't show 'em photographs. I can't say to 'em 'Well y'know when I was twenty-two this this is what happened.'

I can remember sitting with my grandmother on the end, end of her bed and she was just covered with m-m-memorabilia. All that kind of stuff is just gone.

Erm. So – So – you almost. Almost it's like y' have to recreate y-y-y-your own history.

[My three words for the rioters?] Just angry people.

Spot out. The stage in darkness.

The Tricycle Theatre

The Tricycle is proud to be working in the London borough of Brent. During the last 30 years, the Tricycle has enjoyed a unique reputation for high artistic achievement and inclusive education and community work. Open all day, seven days a week, the Tricycle not only houses a 235-seat theatre, a 300-seat cinema, gallery, bar and cafe, but also a painting studio for young people, a rehearsal room and the Creative Space, dedicated to working with children and young people at risk of social exclusion. Its Education Department provides workshops, youth theatres and special performances for 46,000 children and young people annually.

The Tricycle presents an eclectic, multi-cultural programme – in particular plays by black, Irish, Jewish, Asian and South African writers, as well as responding to contemporary issues and events with its ground-breaking 'tribunal plays' and political work. In 1994, it staged the first of its 'tribunal plays': *Half the Picture* by Richard Norton-Taylor and John McGrath (a dramatisation of the Scott arms-to-Iraq inquiry), which was the first play ever to be performed in the Houses of Parliament. The next, marking the 50th anniversary of the 1946 war crimes tribunal, was *Nuremberg*, which was followed by *Srebrenica* – the 1996 UN Rule 61 hearings, which later transferred to the National Theatre and the Belfast Festival. In 1999, the Tricycle's reconstruction of the Stephen Lawrence inquiry, *The Colour of Justice*, transferred to the West End and the National Theatre. In 2003, *Justifying War – Scenes from the Hutton Inquiry* opened at the Tricycle. *Bloody Sunday – Scenes from the Saville Inquiry* followed in 2005 and was also performed at the Abbey in Dublin, Belfast and Derry – it received an Olivier Award for Outstanding Achievement. *Called to Account: The Indictment of Anthony Charles Lynton Blair for the Crime of Aggression Against Iraq – A Hearing* was staged at the Tricycle with evidence from Richard Perle, the Chilean Ambassador to the UN, and ex-cabinet minister Clare Short. All of these plays have been broadcast by the BBC on radio or television, and have together reached audiences of over 34 million people worldwide.

In 2004, *Guantanamo: Honor Bound to Defend Freedom* transferred to the New Ambassadors Theatre in the West End and to the Culture Project in New York. It also played in the Houses of Parliament and on Capitol Hill in Washington, DC. It has since been performed around the world and in the USA through the Guantanamo Reading Project, which develops community productions of readings of the play – 32 performances have already been held in cities across America.

In 2006, the Tricycle received the Evening Standard Special Award for its pioneering work in political theatre.

West End transfers from the Tricycle include *The Amen Corner* by James Baldwin, the Fats Waller musical *Ain't Misbehavin'*, *Guantanamo* and *The Price* by Arthur Miller. Transfers to Broadway include the South African musical *Kat and the Kings* (two 1999 Olivier Awards for Best New Musical and Best Actor – awarded to the entire cast), as well as *Stones in His Pockets* by Marie Jones and *The 39 Steps* adapted by Patrick Barlow (both of which won Olivier Awards in the West End for Best New Comedy).

In the summer of 2009, the Tricycle launched its seven-hour trilogy about Afghanistan, *The Great Game*, which was later nominated for an Olivier Award for Outstanding Achievement. The production returned to the Tricycle in the autumn of 2010 before embarking on a tour of the USA, starting in Washington, then travelling to Minneapolis, Berkeley and New York. In February 2011, the production played two command performances for Pentagon staff, the military, policy-makers and guests in Washington. In 2010, the Tricycle won the Liberty Human Rights Arts Award.

In 2011, The Tricycle presented the World Premiere of *Tactical Questioning: Scenes from the Baha Mousa Inquiry*, edited by Richard Norton-Taylor and directed by Nicolas Kent. The Tricycle also transferred its production of *Broken Glass*, starring Antony Sher and Tara FitzGerald, from the Tricycle Theatre to the Vaudeville Theatre in the West End.

'Britain's leading political playhouse'
The Times, 2011 (leading article)

WWW.OBERONBOOKS.COM

 Follow us on www.twitter.com/@oberonbooks
& www.facebook.com/oberonbook